**Also by Jaroslaw Jankowski**

*Why Are We So Different?*
*Your Guide to the 16 Personality Types*

Why are we so very different from one another?
Why do we organise our lives in such disparate
ways? Why are our modes of assimilating
information so varied? Why are our approaches
to decision-making so diverse? Why are our
forms of relaxing and 'recharging our batteries'
so dissimilar?

*Your Guide to the 16 Personality Types* will help you
to understand both yourselves and other people
better. It will aid you not only in avoiding any
number of traps, but also in making the most of
your personal potential, as well as in taking the
right decisions about your education and career
and in building healthy relationships with others.
The book contains the ID16™© Personality
Test, which will enable you to determine your
own personality type. It also offers
a comprehensive description of each of the
sixteen types.

# The Protector

## Your Guide
## to the ISFJ Personality Type

*The ID16™© Personality Types series*

JAROSLAW JANKOWSKI
M.Ed., EMBA

LOGOS MEDIA

This is a book which can help you exploit your potential more fully, build healthy relationships with other people and make the right decisions about your education and career. However, it should not be considered to be a substitute for expert physiological or psychiatric consultation. Neither the author nor the publisher accept any responsibility whatsoever for any detrimental effects which may result from the inappropriate use of this book.

ID16™© is an independent typology developed by Polish educator and manager Jaroslaw Jankowski and grounded in Carl Gustav Jung's theory. It should not be confused with the personality typologies and tests proposed by other authors or offered by other institutions.

Original title: Twój typ osobowości: Opiekun (ISFJ)
Translated from the Polish by Caryl Swift
Proof reading: Lacrosse | experts in translation
Layout editing by Zbigniew Szalbot

Published by LOGOS MEDIA

Paperback: ISBN 978-83-7981-090-1
EPUB: ISBN 978-83-7981-091-8
MOBI: ISBN 978-83-7981-092-5

# Contents

# Preface

The work in your hands is a compendium of knowledge on the *protector*. It forms part of the *ID16$^{TM©}$ Personality Types* series, which consists of sixteen books on the individual personality types and *Who Are You? The ID16$^{TM©}$ Personality Test*, an introduction to the ID16$^{TM©}$ independent personality typology, which is based on the theory developed by Carl Gustav Jung.

As you explore this book on the *protector*, you will find the answer to a number of crucial questions:

- How do *protectors* think and what do they feel? How do they make decisions? How do they solve problems? What makes them anxious? What do they fear? What irritates them?

- Which personality types are they happy to encounter on their road through life and which ones do they avoid? What kind of friends, life partners and parents do they make? How do others perceive them?
- What are their vocational predispositions? What sort of work environment allows them to function most effectively? Which careers best suit their personality type?
- What are their strengths and what do they need to work on? How can they make the most of their potential and avoid pitfalls?
- Which famous people correspond to the *protector*'s profile?

The book also contains the most essential information about the ID16™© typology.

We sincerely hope that it will help you in coming to know yourself and others better.

# ID16™© and Jungian Personality Typology

ID16™© numbers among what are referred to as Jungian personality typologies, which draw on the theories developed by Carl Gustav Jung (1875-19161), a Swiss psychiatrist and psychologist and a pioneer of the 'depth psychology' approach.

On the basis of many years of research and observation, Jung came to the conclusion that the differences in people's attitudes and preferences are far from random. He developed a concept which is highly familiar to us today: the division of people into extroverts and introverts. In addition, he distinguished four personality functions, which form two opposing pairs: sensing-intuition and thinking-feeling. He also established that one function is dominant in each pair. He became convinced that each and every person's dominant functions are fixed and independent of external conditions and that, together, what they form is a personality type.

In 1938, two American psychiatrists, Horace Gray and Joseph Wheelwright, created the first personality test based on Jung's theories. It was designed to make it possible to determine the dominant functions within the three dimensions described by Jung, namely, **extraversion-introversion**, **sensing-intuition** and **thinking-feeling**. That first test became the inspiration for other researchers. In 1942, again in America, Isabel Briggs Myers and Katherine Briggs began using their own personality test, broadening Gray's and Wheelwright's classic, three-dimensional model to include a fourth: **judging-perceiving**. The majority of subsequent personality typologies and tests drawing on Jung's theories also take that fourth dimension into account. They include the American typology published by David W. Keirsey in 1978 and the personality test developed in the nineteen seventies by Aušra Augustinavičiūtė, a Lithuanian psychologist. Over the following decades, other European researchers followed in their footsteps, creating more four-dimensional personality typologies and tests for use in personal coaching and career counselling.

ID16™© figures among that group. An independent typology developed by Polish educator and manager Jaroslaw Jankowski, it was published in the first decade of the twenty-first century. ID16™© is based on Carl Jung's classic theory and, like other contemporary Jungian typologies, it follows a four-dimensional path, terming those dimensions the **four natural inclinations**. These inclinations are dichotomous in nature and the picture they provide gives us information regarding a person's personality type. Analysis of the first inclination is intended to determine the dominant **source of life energy**, this being either the exterior or the interior world. Analysis of the second inclination defines the dominant **mode of assimilating information**, which occurs via the senses or via intuition. Analysis of the third inclination supplies a description of the **decision-making mode**, where either mind or heart is dominant, while analysis of the fourth inclination produces a definition of the dominant **lifestyle** as either organised or spontaneous. The combination of all these natural inclinations results in **sixteen possible personality types**.

One remarkable feature of the ID16™© typology is its practical dimension. It describes the individual personality types in action – at work, in daily life and in interpersonal relations. It neither concentrates on the internal dynamics of personality nor does it undertake any theoretical attempts at explaining or commenting on invisible, interior processes. The focus is turned more toward the ways in which a given personality type manifests itself externally and how it affects the surrounding world. This emphasis on the social aspect of personality places ID16™© somewhat closer to the previously mentioned typology developed by Aušra Augustinavičiūtė.

Each of the ID16™© personality types is the result of a given person's natural inclinations.

There is nothing evaluative or judgemental about ascribing a person to a given type, though. No particular personality type is 'better' or 'worse' than any other. Each type is quite simply different and each has its own potential strengths and weaknesses. ID16™© makes it possible to identify and describe those differences. It helps us to understand ourselves and discover our place in the world.

Familiarity with our personality profile enables us to make full use of our potential and work on the areas which might cause us trouble. It is an invaluable aid in everyday life, in solving problems, in building healthy relationships with other people and in making decisions relating to our education and careers.

Determining personality is a process which is neither arbitrary nor mechanical in nature. As the 'owner and user' of our personality, each and every one of us is fully capable of defining which type we belong to. The individual's role is thus pivotal. This self-identification can be achieved either by analysing the descriptions of the ID16™© personality types and steadily narrowing down the fields of choice or by taking the short cut provided by the ID16™© Personality Test.[1] The role played by each 'personality user' is equally crucial when it comes to the test, given that the outcome depends entirely on the answers they provide.

---

[1] The test can be found in *Why Are We So Different? Your Guide to the 16 Personality Types* by Jaroslaw Jankowski.

Identifying personality types helps us to know both ourselves and others. Nonetheless, it should not be treated as some kind of future-determining oracle. No personality type can ever justify our weaknesses or poor interpersonal relationships. It might, however, help us to understand their causes!

ID16™© treats personality type not as a static, genetic, pre-determined condition, but as a product of innate and acquired characteristics. As such, it is a concept which neither diminishes free will nor engages in pigeonholing people. What it does is open up new perspectives for us, encouraging us to work on ourselves and indicating the areas where that work is most needed.

# The Protector (ISFJ)

THE ID16™© PERSONALITY TYPOLOGY

## The Personality in a Nutshell

**Life motto:** Your happiness matters to me.

In brief, *protectors* …

are sincere, warm-hearted, unassuming, trustworthy and extraordinarily loyal. With their ability to perceive people's needs and their desire to help them, they will always put others first. Practical, well-organised and gifted with both an eye and a memory for detail, they are responsible, hard-working, patient, persevering and capable of seeing things through to the end.

*Protectors* set great store by tranquillity, stability and friendly relations with others and are skilled at building bridges between people. By the same token, they find conflict and criticism difficult to bear. Given their powerful sense of duty and their constant readiness to come to the aid of others, they can end up being used by people.

## The *protector's* four natural inclinations:

- source of life energy: the interior world
- mode of assimilating information: via the senses
- decision-making mode: the heart
- lifestyle: organised

## Similar personality types:

- the Artist
- the Advocate
- the Presenter

## Statistical data:

- *protectors* constitute between eight and twelve per cent of the global population
- women predominate among *protectors* (70 per cent)
- Sweden is an example of a nation corresponding to the *protector's* profile[2]

---

[2] What this means is not that all the residents of Sweden fall within this personality type, but that Swedish society as a whole possesses a great many of the character traits typical of the *protector*.

## The Four-Letter Code

In terms of Jungian personality typology, the universal four-letter code for the *protector* is ISFJ.

# General character traits

*Protectors* like people! With their interest in the experiences and problems of others and their awareness of their feelings, they are more open to them than any of the other introverted personality types and will spend their entire life scanning their surroundings in search of those who need help.

## As others see them

Other people perceive *protectors* as sincere, kind and always ready to offer a helping hand. They have a reputation for being extremely friendly, tranquil and unassuming. Given their propensity for putting other people first, their inherent need to help them and their ability both to perceive their positive potential and to elicit the best in them, they are widely popular.

## Their attitude to others

A powerful force impels *protectors* to act: their sympathy for those in need, for the poor, for the suffering and for the wronged, and they are ever ready to take them under their wing, offering them practical and emotional support and surrounding them with protection … hence the name for this personality type. With their desire to defend others against hardship, adverse decisions and afflictions, they will spare neither time nor effort in helping them to solve their problems, yet their support is always extremely discreet and tactful; imposing themselves and pursuing recognition is simply not the way they operate.

## Organisational modes

*Protectors* keep themselves to themselves and are sparing with words. Hard-working, responsible and well-organised, they have a head for detail and bear in mind the kind of minutiae that escape the notice of others. This is a character trait which also applies to their interpersonal relationships; even after years have gone by, they will have a precise recall of exactly what someone said or of a specific gesture or facial expression.

They have a genuine faith in other people and are able to spot the best in them. Prizing harmonious collaboration, an open, warm and friendly atmosphere, security and stability, they are driven by their sense of good and strive for concord and unity. Unforeseen situations and sudden change upset them; they are happiest when everything happens according to plan. In general, they have a fondness for tradition and, preferring tried and tested modes of action which have survived the test of time, they approach new solutions with a degree of mistrust. Nonetheless, if they can see that employing them will produce evident benefits, then they are inclined to accept them.

Wastefulness goes against the grain with *protectors*. Thrifty by nature, they give due consideration to the uncertainties of the future and thus tend to put money aside 'for a rainy day'.

## Thinking

*Protectors* build their own unique 'internal database', storing information concerning events affecting themselves and others. They are able to connect new facts with previous experiences and have a clear picture of what the world and relationships between people should be like. It is this which forms their reference point; their activities are geared towards turning their vision into reality. By the same token, being practitioners by nature, they will rarely concern themselves with abstract theories.

Encounters with opinions which differ from their own are something of a problem for them, causing them an enormous sense of unease and disrupting their interior calm, leading to a response which will usually be an attempt either to reconcile the disparate views or, at the very least, to reduce the divide between them.

## Communication

*Protectors* are excellent listeners and are perceived by others as wonderful conversationalists, even when they actually say very little. They are happiest in intimate surroundings and prefer their conversations to be *tête-à-tête*, since talking to just one person allows them to give all their attention to whatever is being discussed. On the whole, though, they will struggle to establish any kind of meaningful connection with people who are chaotic, who go through life in a permanent state of absent-mindedness, who are incapable of punctuality or who are simply unreliable.

Criticising others openly is difficult for them, as is expressing their disapproval of something publicly. Indeed, some people resent them for making unfavourable remarks behind people's backs rather than directly to the person concerned.

Given their sense of the continuity of processes, their orderliness and the fact that they like to follow the proper sequence when they do things, *protectors* prefer to have time to think and ready themselves when faced with taking part in a discussion or giving a presentation. The outcome will usually be a speech or talk which is composed and cool-headed, but powerful enough to move the listeners.

## Decisions

*Protectors* steer well clear of risk and of the unknown and unfamiliar. With their dislike of haste, they approach decisions carefully, step by step, needing time in order to give calm consideration to the various options available to them and often making notes and carrying out a written analysis of those possibilities while turning things over in their minds. They also give thought both to the way a given decision will affect other people and to how they will perceive it. The final result of these deliberations will be based on hard facts and previous experience.

In general, *protectors* have a very highly developed sense of duty and responsibility. Seldom will they refuse when asked to help or do someone a favour, a character trait which means that they are often used by others and frequently find themselves overburdened. However, even in situations of that kind, they rarely resort to complaints or accusations, not wishing to jeopardise their relationships with others by speaking out.

## Aesthetics

*Protectors* possess an excellent spatial imagination and the ability to arrange their surroundings in a way which is both functional and yet still reveals their sensitivity to beauty. As a result, their homes and workstations are distinctive not only for their orderliness and the highly practical way in which they are organised, but also for the tastefulness of their décor, to say nothing of their immense cosiness … people are always happy to spend time in a space created by a *protector*.

They set great store by other people's anniversaries and birthdays, showing their liking through kind gestures and happy surprises. With their skill for identifying what fills others with enthusiasm, what they enjoy and what they need, even the smallest of the gifts given by a *protector* will always be a source of enormous joy, being not only tasteful, but also highly thoughtful and wholly suited to the recipient.

## Leisure

*Protectors* are incapable of relaxing unless they know that there are no uncompleted tasks awaiting them; and so, given their propensity for taking on myriad responsibilities, it is hardly surprising that they have very little in the way of what they would deem to be free time! This state of affairs is further exacerbated by the fact that their concept of 'free time' diverges markedly from the norm; to a *protector*, it equates with 'time to help my nearest and dearest' and 'time to help my friends and acquaintances'. It is rare, indeed, to see them doing something simply for their own pleasure.

## Socially

The ties which bind *protectors* to others are highly particular and personal in nature, since they see them not only as colleagues, superiors, subordinates, clients or people in their care, but also as individuals who have their own world, their own enthusiasms, their own feelings and their own emotions. What lies at the heart of their relationships is the notion of service and their longing to feel useful.

They also have a need for confirmation that they have done a good job and that their opinions are shared by others. Although they are genuinely embarrassed by praise, they find sheer indifference on the part of others very hard to bear and are equally as disheartened by open criticism. In stressful situations, they will start conjuring up a range of black scenarios, imagining all sorts of misfortunes which might be lying in wait for them, losing faith in their own abilities and seeing the future through gloom-tinted glasses.

Only too happy to come to the aid of others, they will often give no sign that they are grappling with problems of their own, preferring not to burden other people with their troubles. They tend not to express their dissatisfaction or discontent outwardly, and are inclined to bottle up their emotions. However, having kept them firmly suppressed for a long time, they might then give way to an uncontrolled explosion, much to the astonishment of those around them.

## Amongst friends

*Protectors* are genuinely interested in the lives and problems of their friends. In their case, one thing which will never serve as an instrument for self-advertising, for instance, or as a tool for building their career, is friendship. Its bonds are a crucial aspect of their world and will normally endure throughout their lives, since they take them as seriously as any of their other responsibilities.

Their friends appreciate them because they are not focused on themselves, their interest is both genuine and wholehearted and they can always be counted on. They also value them for their ability to perceive the needs and problems of others.

A positive attitude towards others and the ability to identify something of worth in everyone are both common character traits among *protectors* and mean that they are happy in the company of people representing all sixteen of the personality types. However, they most frequently strike up a friendship with *artists*, *advocates*, *mentors* and other *protectors* and, most rarely, with *innovators*, *logicians* and *directors*.

After periods of intensive activity or a lengthy time spent with a group of people, they need solitude and tranquillity in order to gather their thoughts and 'recharge their batteries'. However, in no way at all is this a manifestation of antipathy towards others.

## As life partners

The axis of the *protector's* world is their family. In general, they set great store by traditional values and are both highly devoted to those closest to them and solicitous of their welfare, security and well-being. They also strive for good and healthy relationships and are capable of investing enormous energy in that cause. Their feelings run very deep, even though this intensity may not always be perceived via 'the naked ear', since they tend to express it not through words, but via concrete actions and warm gestures of affection. They themselves attach enormous value to any and every manifestation of fondness, feeling and gratitude from their partner. Highly faithful and uncommonly loyal, they take their responsibilities extremely seriously and their relationships tend to last a lifetime.

Their relationship with their partner is their highest priority and, even when it has soured beyond mending or is harmful or toxic, they face a struggle in trying to break free of it and, if their partner leaves them, they have equal difficulty in coming to terms with that. In either situation, they tend to blame themselves, seeking to identify their own mistakes and shortcomings. Given that their unselfishness and focus on others is part of their nature, they are often used and, more to the point, will generally accept that state of affairs. They cope badly in situations of conflict and will do anything they can to avoid touching on thorny subjects, preferring to remain silent about problems, either bearing them patiently or pretending that they do not exist.

The natural candidates for a *protector's* life partner are people of a personality type akin to their own: *artists*, *advocates* and *presenters*. Building mutual understanding and harmonious relations will be easier in a union of that kind. Nonetheless, experience has taught us that people are also capable of creating happy and successful relationships despite what would seem to be an evident typological incompatibility. Moreover, the differences between two partners can lend added dynamics to a relationship and engender personal development.

## As parents

*Protectors* make highly responsible parents, tending to the needs of their children and taking their parental responsibilities extremely seriously. Desiring to bring their offspring up to be independent and responsible adults, they believe in the necessity of teaching them to behave appropriately from the earliest years; as a result, their parenting style is not only devoted, but also decisive. In general, they run their homes along lucid principles, thanks to which their children both know how they should behave and enjoy a sense of security. However, *protectors* themselves sometimes have problems with enforcing those selfsame rules and taking the requisite disciplinary action – before they punish a child for behaving badly, they first need to convince themselves that doing so will be for the best.

Their offspring often take advantage of their *protector* parent's devotion, operating on the assumption that they will do anything for them. When their adult children face problems, they are inclined to seek the fault in their own parenting errors. In general, though, they are following a false trail, since they do an excellent job, providing a secure childhood and a wonderful home filled with warmth. As adults, their children appreciate them for their devotion, care and for instilling them with healthy principles and a sense of responsibility.

## Work and career paths

*Protectors* are extremely persevering and ready both to devote themselves to what they are doing and to give up their own pleasures in favour of the task in hand. They are happiest in jobs which are rooted in helping others or supporting those who are unable to cope themselves and they enjoy tasks that allow them to solve human problems. When they work in a business, they love advising and assisting people to select the product or service which best suits their requirements and, if they work for a social institution, they will always be dedicated in giving their care to those in need of help.

### Environment

In general terms, the awareness of belonging to a larger group or community that they can identify with is important to *protectors* and they also prefer companies or institutions which establish structures designed to help ease tensions amongst the staff. When they are working on a task, they require moments of solitude and calm in order to think through what they have to do and prepare for it away from the daily hustle and bustle. However, if they can see the necessity for team work, they will willingly get involved, although they will feel more at ease in a small group of no more than a few people. They bring a warm and pleasant atmosphere to the team, are always supportive of the other members and are often instrumental in helping the group achieve a consensus.

When it comes to approach, they prefer regular, well-prepared meetings where the time, date and agenda are all established in advance. Surprises, improvisation and unexpected discussions of problems, where they have no opportunity to think things over first, are anathema to them.

## Tasks

Capable of seeing things through to the end, *protectors* derive tremendous satisfaction from a job well done. With their highly meticulous natures and ability to focus on detail, they see nothing tedious in routine activities and their reliability, friendly attitude and willingness to extend a helping hand to others all make them sought-after employees. They like clearly defined tasks and much prefer to work on things they are familiar with and which allow them to draw on their experience. When confronted by something new, they need more time to take it on board than many other people do. However, once they have thoroughly familiarised themselves with it, they will accomplish it to a greater exactitude than most.

*Protectors* make uncommonly loyal staff members and, with their own ability to give their all in pursuit of accomplishing their employer's aims, they find those who consciously neglect their duties absolutely incomprehensible.

## Preferences

Instructions, rules and regulations are meat and drink to *protectors*, who like to know what they have to do and how they should do it and are fully capable of adapting themselves completely to existing guidelines and prescripts. At a loss in situations where they have to come up with something new or move into the unknown, they cope just as badly when circumstances deprive them of the chance to refer to concrete instructions or call on previous experience and either demand that they improvise or force them into making a rapid decision. Organisational changes, new procedures and transformations also knock them off their feet; they prefer a stable environment where things all stay very much the same.

## Views on workplace hierarchy

*Protectors* appreciate well-organised superiors who are capable of spotting the devotion and dedication of those they supervise and who provide them with the support they need. They favour clear guidelines, concrete aims and comprehensible rules which apply to all the staff.

Although they like to have an influence on the course of affairs and the decision-making process, they make unwilling leaders. They would rather work behind the lines, supporting the 'high command', a *modus operandi* which enables them to avoid the necessity of disciplining people, calling their attention to shortcomings or solving conflicts, and also absolves them of responsibility for implementing unpopular decisions.

Those *protectors* who do become leaders introduce extremely exacting standards and are rigorous about maintaining a high level of efficacy and efficiency, demonstrating zero tolerance for wastefulness. They set out clear, concrete aims for the people they supervise and then provide the support they need in order to achieve them. On the other hand, when forced to hold an 'unpleasant conversation' with one of their personnel, the *protector* will often end up far more exhausted and stressed than the staff member concerned. Given that they feel ill-at-ease when telling someone to do something, issuing instructions is another problem area for them, as is the very delegation of duties itself; indeed, they themselves will often carry out tasks which should, by rights, be handed off to their staff. This, in turn, produces an undesirable outcome, with the *protector* becoming overworked and fatigued, while their staff are deprived of the opportunity to learn, develop and improve their skills.

## Professions

Knowledge of our own personality profile and natural preferences provides us with invaluable help in choosing the optimal path in our professional careers. Experience has shown that, while *protectors* are perfectly able to work and find fulfilment in a range of fields, their personality type naturally predisposes them to the following fields and professions:

- acting
- administrator
- advisor
- bookkeeper
- clergy
- the construction industry
- designer
- education officer
- entrepreneur
- estate agent
- farmer
- gardener
- human resources
- interior designer
- insurance agent
- librarian
- manager
- medical technician
- musician
- office manager
- paramedic
- personal trainer

- physician
- physiotherapist
- psychologist
- sales assistant
- sports trainer
- social welfare
- teacher
- therapist
- vet

# Potential strengths and weaknesses

Like any other personality type, *protectors* have their potential strengths and weaknesses and this potential can be cultivated in a variety of ways. *Protectors'* personal happiness and professional fulfilment depend on whether they make the most of the 'pluses' offered by their personality type and face up to its inherent dangers. Here, then, is a SUMMARY of those 'pluses' and dangers:

## Potential strengths

*Protectors* are uncommonly loyal and take their responsibilities extremely seriously. Hard-working, persevering and patient, they are always ready to commit themselves to the full, sparing neither time nor energy in fulfilling their tasks and seeing things through to the end, undiscouraged by obstacles and setbacks. They are open to others, genuinely interested in them and capable of perceiving their feelings, enthusiasms and emotions. Their attitude is friendly and they are discreet, loyal and geared towards the needs of other people, putting them first and giving no real thought to themselves.

Other people feel good in their company, since they are excellent listeners and offer practical and emotional support to those in need of help or caught in the midst of a crisis. Consensus is one of their watchwords; they create a healthy, constructive atmosphere and will always strive to build bridges between people and assist them in reaching a compromise.

Their spatial imagination is as superb as is their sense of practicality. Orderliness comes as naturally to them as breathing, they see nothing tedious about carrying out routine activities and have no difficulty in following complex procedures. Given their natural talent for organisation, their head for detail and their ability to keep in mind the kind of minutiae that escape the notice of others, they make excellent resource managers.

## Potential weaknesses

Being oriented towards serving others and rather lacking in assertiveness, *protectors* are sometimes neglectful of their own needs and backward in defending their own interests. Indeed, they often find themselves incapable of articulating their expectations or voicing their opinions, particularly when they veer towards the critical, and are equally as unable to end toxic and damaging relationships. Their tendency to remain silent on thorny subjects and avoid difficult conversations, even when they are essential, renders them vulnerable to deceit, manipulation and being used by others. They struggle just as much with expressing their feelings, which run deep and intense; indeed, their constant suppression of negative emotions will sometimes lead to uncontrolled and destructive explosions.

They find it difficult to cope in fields of activity which are completely new to them and, being rather inflexible, they quickly find themselves completely at sea in situations demanding swift decisions or improvisation and tend to be knocked off their feet by crises. They also have a problem with delegating duties and responsibilities, as well as tendency to do too much for others and help them whether they like it or not.

When it comes to viewing reality, *protectors* frequently struggle to look at the bigger picture. Understanding other people's views when they conflict with their own also comes hard to them; indeed, simply encountering those opinions can cause them deep discomfort. Inclined to perceive their own ideas as exclusively 'right', they are prone to negating anything which goes against their convictions and discarding it prematurely. They have no real mechanisms for handling criticism either, and frequently take unfavourable opinions of their outlook or activities as a personal defeat and a sign that they have disappointed people.

## Personal development

*Protectors'* personal development depends on the extent to which they make use of their natural potential and surmount the dangers inherent in their personality type. What follows are some practical tips which, together, form a specific guide that we might call *The Protector's Ten Commandments*.

## Stop fearing other people's ideas and opinions

Being open to the viewpoints of others is not synonymous with discarding your own. Stop fearing ideas and opinions which are different from yours. Before you reject them, give them some consideration and try to understand them.

## Look at problems from a wider perspective

Try to look at problems in a wider context, from various angles ... and through other people's eyes. Reach for their opinions, give thought to various points of view. Take all the different sides of the matter into consideration.

## Learn to say 'no'

When you disagree with something, why be afraid to speak out? When you are simply unable to take yet another task onto your shoulders, then just say so. Learn to say 'no', particularly when you feel that someone is abusing your help or trying to land you with everything!

## Stop being afraid of new experiences

Try something new every week or every month. Go somewhere you have never been before, talk to people you have never got to know before, undertake tasks you have never done before. It will give you a host of valuable ideas and mean that you start seeing the world from a wider perspective.

## Stop being afraid of conflict

Conflicts do arise sometimes, even in our closest circles. They need not necessarily be destructive, though. In fact, they very often help us to uncover problems and solve them! So, when they emerge, stop hiding your head in the sand and, instead, express your point of view and feelings about the situation openly.

## Leave some things to take their natural course

There is no way you can have everything under your personal control. There is no way you can manage to be in command of every single thing. Leave those less important matters to take their natural course. You will save energy and avoid frustration.

## Stop doing everything for others

You may thirst to help people, but if you do everything for them, they will never learn anything new for themselves and you will be perpetually overburdened. When you give others a helping hand, let them take responsibility for their own lives, make their own mistakes and draw their own conclusions from them for the future.

## Accept help from others

You operate in the belief that you should be helping other people and that others usually seek support from you. Well, when you have a problem, turn the tables on that assumption! Stop hesitating, ask others for their help and then grasp the hand they offer!

## Stop fearing criticism

Quell your fear of expressing your own critical opinions and of accepting criticism from others. Criticism can be constructive. There is no law which says that it has to mean attacking people or undermining their worth.

## Be kinder to yourself

Try to help yourself with the same solicitude that you give to the happiness and well-being of others. Be more understanding of yourself. Try to get away from your responsibilities and duties once in a while and do something for the sheer pleasure, relaxation and fun of it.

# Well-known figures

Below is a list of some well-known people who match the *protector's* profile:

- **Alfred, Lord Tennyson** (1809-1892); one of England's most popular poets, whose works include *The Lady of Shallot* and *Idylls of the King*, the most famous nineteenth-century adaptation of the legend of King Arthur and the Knights of the Round Table. He served as Poet Laureate for more than forty years.

- **Charles Dickens** (1812-1870); an English author regarded as the greatest literary colossus of the Victorian era. His novels, such as *Oliver Twist*, contained a powerful vein of social criticism and moral critique. He was also a prolific writer of short stories, the editor of a weekly journal and a vigorous campaigner for social reform.
- **Louisa May Alcott** (1832-1888); an American writer and pioneer of women's literature, she served as a volunteer nurse during the Civil War.
- **Teresa of Calcutta, MC** (Agnes Gonxha Bojaxhiu; 1910-1997); an Albanian-born, Roman Catholic nun and missionary more commonly known as Mother Teresa, she founded the Missionaries of Charity and spent most of her life engaged in humanitarian work in India. A holder of the Nobel Peace Prize, she was beatified in 2003.
- **William Shatner** (born in 1931); a Canadian screen actor whose filmography includes the *Star Trek* TV series and films, he is also a director, producer, writer, singer and comedian.
- **Connie Sellecca** (born in 1955); an American screen actress whose filmography includes *The Wild Stallion*.
- **Diana, Princess of Wales** (*née* Lady Diana Francis Spencer; 1961-1997); the first wife of Charles, Prince of Wales and

the mother of his two sons, she was deeply involved in charitable activities.

- **Michael Jordan** (born in 1963); a retired American basketball player, he is considered the greatest of all time in the discipline and is now an entrepreneur.
- **Kiefer Sutherland** (born in 1966); a British-born, Canadian screen actor whose filmography includes *A Few Good Men*, he is also a producer and director.
- **Rose McGowan** (born in 1973); an American screen actress whose filmography includes the *Charmed* TV series.
- **Tori Spelling** (Victoria Davey Spelling; born in 1973); an American screen actress whose filmography includes the *Beverly Hills, 90210* TV series, she is also an author.
- **Sarah Polley** (born in 1979); a Canadian screen actress whose filmography includes *The Secret Life of Words*, she is also a director, a screenwriter and a social and political activist.

# The ID16™ Personality Types in a Nutshell

## The Administrator (ESTJ)

Life motto: We'll get the job done!

*Administrators* are hard-working, responsible and extremely loyal. Energetic and decisive, they value order, stability, security and clear rules. They are matter-of-fact and businesslike, logical, rational and practical and possess the capability to assimilate large amounts of detailed information.

Superb organisers, they are intolerant of ineffectuality, wastefulness and slothfulness. True to their convictions and direct in their contact with others, they present their point of view decisively and openly express critical opinions, sometimes hurting other people as a result.

## The *administrator*'s four natural inclinations:

- source of life energy: the exterior world
- mode of assimilating information: via the senses
- decision-making mode: the mind
- lifestyle: organised

## Similar personality types:

- the Animator
- the Inspector
- the Practitioner

## Statistical data:

- *administrators* constitute between ten and thirteen per cent of the global community
- men predominate among *administrators* (60 per cent)
- the United States is an example of a nation corresponding to the *administrator's* profile[3]

## Find out more!

*The Administrator. Your Guide to the ESTJ Personality Type* by Jaroslaw Jankowski

---

[3] What this means is not that all the residents of the USA fall within this personality type, but that American society as a whole possesses a great many of the character traits typical of the *administrator*.

# The Advocate (ESFJ)

Life motto: How can I help you?

*Advocates* are well-organised, energetic and enthusiastic. Practical, responsible and conscientious, they are sincere and exceptionally gregarious.

*Advocates* are perceptive of human feelings, emotions and needs. They value harmony and find criticism and conflict difficult to bear. With their sensitivity to any and every manifestation of injustice, prejudice or detriment to another, they are genuinely interested in other people's problems and take real delight in helping them and tending to their needs, while often neglecting their own. They have a tendency to do everything for others and can be vulnerable to manipulation.

## The *advocate*'s four natural inclinations:

- source of life energy: the exterior world
- mode of assimilating information: via the senses
- decision-making mode: the heart
- lifestyle: organised

## Similar personality types:

- the Presenter
- the Protector
- the Artist

## Statistical data:

- *advocates* constitute between ten and thirteen per cent of the global community
- women predominate among *advocates* (70 per cent)
- Canada is an example of a nation corresponding to the *advocate's* profile

## Find out more!

*The Advocate. Your Guide to the ESFJ Personality Type* by Jaroslaw Jankowski


# The Animator (ESTP)

Life motto: Let's DO something!

*Animators* are energetic, active and enterprising. Fond of the company of others, they have the ability to enjoy the moment and are spontaneous, flexible and open to change.

*Animators* are inspirers and instigators, spurring others to act. Being logical, rational and pragmatic realists, they are wearied by abstract concepts and solutions for the future. Their focus is on solving concrete problems in the here and now. They have difficulties with organising and planning and can be impulsive, acting first and thinking later.

## The *animator's* four natural inclinations:

- source of life energy: the exterior world
- mode of assimilating information: via the senses

- decision-making mode: the mind
- lifestyle: spontaneous

## Similar personality types:

- the Administrator
- the Practitioner
- the Inspector

## Statistical data:

- *animators* constitute between six and ten per cent of the global community
- men predominate among *animators* (60 per cent)
- Australia is an example of a nation corresponding to the *animator's* profile

## Find out more!

*The Animator. Your Guide to the ESTP Personality Type* by Jaroslaw Jankowski

# The Artist (ISFP)

Life motto: Let's create something!

*Artists* are sensitive, creative and original, with a sense of the aesthetic and natural artistic talents. Independent in character, they follow their own system of values and are optimistic in outlook, with a positive approach to life and an ability to enjoy the moment.

Helping others is a source of joy to them. They find abstract theories tedious and would rather create reality than talk about it, although starting on something new comes more easily to them than finishing what they have already started. They have difficulty in voicing their own desires and needs.

## The *artist's* four natural inclinations:

- source of life energy: the interior world
- mode of assimilating information: via the senses
- decision-making mode: the heart
- lifestyle: spontaneous

## Similar personality types:

- the Protector
- the Presenter
- the Advocate

## Statistical data:

- *artists* constitute between six and nine per cent of the global community
- women predominate among *artists* (60 per cent)
- China is an example of a nation corresponding to the *artist's* profile

## Find out more!

*The Artist. Your Guide to the ISFP Personality Type* by Jaroslaw Jankowski

# The Counsellor (ENFJ)

Life motto: My friends are my world

*Counsellors* are optimistic, enthusiastic and quick-witted. Courteous and tactful, they have an extraordinary gift for empathy and find joy in acting for the good of others, with no thought of themselves. They have the ability to influence other people, inspiring them, eliciting their hidden potential and giving them faith in their own powers. Radiating warmth, they draw others to them and often help them in solving their personal problems.

*Counsellors* can be over-trusting and have a tendency to view the world through rose-tinted glasses. With their focus on other people, they often forget about their own needs.

## The *counsellor's* four natural inclinations:

- source of life energy: the exterior world
- mode of assimilating information: intuition
- decision-making mode: the heart
- lifestyle: organised

## Similar personality types:

- the Enthusiast
- the Mentor
- the Idealist

## Statistical data:

- *counsellors* constitute between three and five per cent of the global community
- women predominate among *counsellors* (80 per cent)
- France is an example of a nation corresponding to the *counsellor's* profile

## Find out more!

*The Counsellor. Your Guide to the ENFJ Personality Type* by Jaroslaw Jankowski

# The Director (ENTJ)

Life motto: I'll tell you what you need to do.

*Directors* are independent, active and decisive. Rational, logical and creative, when they analyse problems they look at the wider picture and are able to foresee the future consequences of human activities. They are characterised by optimism and a healthy sense of their own worth and are capable of transforming theoretical concepts into concrete, practical plans of action.

Visionaries, mentors and organisers, *directors* possess natural leadership skills. Their powerful personalities and direct and critical style can often have an intimidating effect, causing them problems in their interpersonal relationships.

## The *director's* four natural inclinations:

- source of life energy: the exterior world

- mode of assimilating information: intuition
- decision-making mode: the mind
- lifestyle: organised

## Similar personality types:
- the Innovator
- the Strategist
- the Logician

## Statistical data:
- *directors* constitute between two and five per cent of the global community
- men predominate among *directors* (70 per cent)
- Holland is an example of a nation corresponding to the *director's* profile

## Find out more!

*The Director. Your Guide to the ENTJ Personality Type* by Jaroslaw Jankowski

# The Enthusiast (ENFP)

Life motto: We'll manage!

*Enthusiasts* are energetic, enthusiastic and optimistic. Capable of enjoying life and looking ahead to the future, they are dynamic, quick-witted and creative. They have a liking for people in general, value honest and genuine relationships and are warm, sincere and emotional. Criticism is something they handle badly. With their gift for empathy and ability to perceive people's needs, feelings and motives, they both inspire others and infect them with their own enthusiasm.

They love to be at the centre of events and are flexible and capable of improvising. Their inclination leads towards idealistic notions. Being easily distracted, they have problems with seeing things through to the end.

## The *enthusiast's* four natural inclinations:

- source of life energy: the exterior world
- mode of assimilating information: intuition
- decision-making mode: the heart
- lifestyle: spontaneous

## Similar personality types:

- the Counsellor
- the Idealist
- the Mentor

## Statistical data:

- *enthusiasts* constitute between five and eight per cent of the global community
- women predominate among *enthusiasts* (60 per cent)
- Italy is an example of a nation corresponding to the *enthusiast's* profile

## Find out more!

*The Enthusiast. Your Guide to the ENFP Personality Type* by Jaroslaw Jankowski

# The Idealist (INFP)

Life motto: We CAN live differently.

*Idealists* are sensitive, loyal, and creative. Living in accordance with the values they hold is of immense importance to them and they both manifest an interest in the reality of the spirit and delve deeply into the mysteries of life. Wrapped up in the world's problems and open to the needs of other people, they prize harmony and balance.

*Idealists* are romantic; not only are they able to show love, but they also need warmth and affection themselves. With their outstanding ability to read other people's feelings and emotions, they build healthy, profound and enduring relationships. They feel that they are on very shaky ground in situations of conflict and have no real resistance to stress and criticism.

## The *idealist's* four natural inclinations:

- source of life energy: the interior world
- mode of assimilating information: intuition
- decision-making mode: the heart
- lifestyle: spontaneous

## Similar personality types:

- the Mentor
- the Enthusiast
- the Counsellor

## Statistical data:

- *idealists* constitute between one and four per cent of the global community
- women predominate among *idealists* (60 per cent)
- Thailand is an example of a nation corresponding to the *idealist's* profile

## Find out more!

*The Idealist. Your Guide to the INFP Personality Type* by Jaroslaw Jankowski

# The Innovator (ENTP)

Life motto: How about trying a different approach…?

*Innovators* are inventive, original and independent. Optimistic, energetic and enterprising, they are people of action who love being at the centre of events and solving 'insoluble' problems. Their thoughts are turned to the future and they are curious about the world and visionary by nature. Open to new concepts and ideas, they enjoy new experiences and experiments and have the ability to identify the connections between separate events.

*Innovators* are spontaneous, communicative and self-assured. However, they tend to overestimate their own possibilities and have problems with seeing things through to the end. They are also inclined to be impatient and to take risks.

## The *innovator's* four natural inclinations:

- source of life energy: the exterior world
- mode of assimilating information: intuition
- decision-making mode: the mind
- lifestyle: spontaneous

## Similar personality types:

- the Director
- the Logician
- the Strategist

## Statistical data:

- *innovators* constitute between three and five per cent of the global community
- men predominate among *innovators* (70 per cent)
- Israel is an example of a nation corresponding to the *innovator's* profile

## Find out more!

*The Innovator. Your Guide to the ENTP Personality Type* by Jaroslaw Jankowski

# The Inspector (ISTJ)

Life motto: *Duty first.*

*Inspectors* are people who can always be counted on. Well-mannered, punctual, reliable, conscientious and responsible, when they give their word, they keep it. Being analytical, methodical, systematic and logical by nature, they tend be seen as serious, cold and reserved. They prize calm, stability and order, have no fondness for change and like clear principles and concrete rules.

*Inspectors* are hard-working, persevering and capable of seeing things through to the end. As perfectionists, they try to exercise control over everything within their sphere and are sparing in their praise. They also underrate the importance of other people's feelings and emotions.

## The *inspector's* four natural inclinations:

- source of life energy: the interior world
- mode of assimilating information: via the senses
- decision-making mode: the mind
- lifestyle: organised

## Similar personality types:

- the Practitioner
- the Administrator
- the Animator

## Statistical data:

- *inspectors* constitute between six and ten per cent of the global community
- men predominate among *inspectors* (60 per cent)
- Switzerland is an example of a nation corresponding to the *inspector's* profile

## Find out more!

*The Inspector. Your Guide to the ISTJ Personality Type* by Jaroslaw Jankowski

# The Logician (INTP)

Life motto: Above all else, seek to discover the truths about the world.

*Logicians* are original, resourceful and creative. With a love for solving problems of a theoretical nature, they are analytical, quick-witted, enthusiastically disposed towards new concepts and have the ability to connect individual phenomena, educing general rules and theories from them. Logical, exact and inquiring, they are quick to spot incoherence and inconsistency.

Logicians are independent, sceptical of existing solutions and authorities, tolerant and open to new challenges. When immersed in thought, they will sometimes lose touch with the outside world.

## The *logician's* four natural inclinations:

- source of life energy: the interior world

- mode of assimilating information: intuition
- decision-making mode: the mind
- lifestyle: spontaneous

## Similar personality types:

- the Strategist
- the Innovator
- the Director

## Statistical data:

- *logicians* constitute between two and three per cent of the global community;
- men predominate among *logicians* (80 per cent)
- India is an example of a nation corresponding to the *logician's* profile

## Find out more!

*The Logician. Your Guide to the INTP Personality Type* by Jaroslaw Jankowski


# The Mentor (INFJ)

Life motto: The world CAN be a better place!

*Mentors* are creative and sensitive. With their gaze fixed firmly on the future, they spot opportunities and potential imperceptible to others. Idealists and visionaries, they are geared towards helping people and are conscientious, responsible and, at one and the same time, courteous, caring and friendly. They strive to understand the mechanisms governing the world and view problems from a wide perspective.

Superb listeners and observers, *mentors* are characterised by their extraordinary empathy, intuition and trust of people and are capable of reading the feelings and emotions of others. They find criticism and conflict difficult to bear and can come across as enigmatic.

## The *mentor's* four natural inclinations:

- source of life energy: the interior world
- mode of assimilating information: intuition
- decision-making mode: the heart
- lifestyle: organised

## Similar personality types:

- the Idealist
- the Counsellor
- the Enthusiast

## Statistical data:

- *mentors* constitute one per cent of the global community and are the most rarely occurring of the sixteen personality types
- women predominate among *mentors* (80 per cent)
- Norway is an example of a nation corresponding to the *mentor's* profile

**Find out more!**

*The Mentor. Your Guide to the INFJ Personality Type* by Jaroslaw Jankowski

# The Practitioner (ISTP)

Life motto: Actions speak louder than words.

*Practitioners* are optimistic and spontaneous, with a positive approach to life. Reserved and independent, they hold true to their personal convictions and view external principles and norms with scepticism. They find abstract concepts and solutions for the future tiresome and would far rather roll up their sleeves and get to work on solving tangible and concrete problems.

Adapting well to new places and situations, they enjoy fresh challenges and risks and are capable of keeping a cool head in the face of threats and danger. Their general reticence and extreme reserve when it comes to expressing their opinions mean that other people may often find them impenetrable.

## The *practitioner's* four natural inclinations:

- source of life energy: the interior world
- mode of assimilating information: via the senses
- decision-making mode: the mind
- lifestyle: spontaneous

## Similar personality types:

- the Inspector
- the Animator
- the Administrator

## Statistical data:

- *practitioners* constitute between six and nine per cent of the global community
- men predominate among *practitioners* (60 per cent)
- Singapore is an example of a nation corresponding to the *practitioner's* profile

## Find out more!

*The Practitioner. Your Guide to the ISTP Personality Type* by Jaroslaw Jankowski

# The Presenter (ESFP)

Life motto: Now is the perfect moment!

*Presenters* are optimistic, energetic and outgoing, with the ability to enjoy life and have fun to the full. Practical, flexible and spontaneous at one and the same time, they enjoy change and new experiences, coping badly with solitude, stagnation and routine.

With their liking for being at the centre of attention, they are natural-born actors and their speaking abilities arouse the interest and enthusiasm of their listeners. Focused as they are on the present moment, they will sometimes lose sight of their long-term aims and can also have problems with foreseeing the consequences of their actions.

## The *presenter's* four natural inclinations:

- source of life energy: the exterior world
- mode of assimilating information: via the senses
- decision-making mode: the heart
- lifestyle: spontaneous

## Similar personality types:

- the Advocate
- the Artist
- the Protector

## Statistical data:

- *presenters* constitute between eight and thirteen per cent of the global community
- women predominate among *presenters* (60 per cent)
- Brazil is an example of a nation corresponding to the *presenter's* profile

## Find out more!

*The Presenter. Your Guide to the ESFP Personality Type* by Jaroslaw Jankowski

# The Protector (ISFJ)

Life motto: Your happiness matters to me.

*Protectors* are sincere, warm-hearted, unassuming, trustworthy and extraordinarily loyal. With their ability to perceive people's needs and their desire to help them, they will always put others first. Practical, well-organised and gifted with both an eye and a memory for detail, they are responsible, hard-working, patient, persevering and capable of seeing things through to the end.

*Protectors* set great store by tranquillity, stability and friendly relations with others and are skilled at building bridges between people. By the same token, they find conflict and criticism difficult to bear. Given their powerful sense of duty and their constant readiness to come to the aid of others, they can end up being used by people.

## The *protector's* four natural inclinations:

- source of life energy: the interior world
- mode of assimilating information: via the senses
- decision-making mode: the heart
- lifestyle: organised

## Similar personality types:

- the Artist
- the Advocate
- the Presenter

## Statistical data:

- *protectors* constitute between eight and twelve per cent of the global population
- women predominate among *protectors* (70 per cent)
- Sweden is an example of a nation corresponding to the *protector's* profile

## Find out more!

*The Protector. Your Guide to the ISFJ Personality Type* by Jaroslaw Jankowski

# The Strategist (INTJ)

Life motto: I can certainly improve this.

*Strategists* are independent and outstandingly individualistic, with an immense seam of inner energy. Creative, inventive and resourceful, others perceive them as competent, self-assured and, at one and the same time, distant and enigmatic. No matter what they turn their attention to, they will always look at the bigger picture and they have a driving urge to improve the world around them and set it in order.

Well-organised, responsible, critical and demanding, they are difficult to knock off balance – and just as hard to please to the full. Reading the emotions and feelings of others is something they find very problematic.

## The *strategist's* four natural inclinations:

- source of life energy: the interior world
- mode of assimilating information: intuition
- decision-making mode: the mind
- lifestyle: organised

## Similar personality types:

- the Logician
- the Director
- the Innovator

## Statistical data:

- *strategists* constitute between one and two per cent of the global community
- men predominate among *strategists* (80 per cent)
- Finland is an example of a nation corresponding to the *strategist's* profile

## Find out more!

*The Strategist. Your Guide to the INTJ Personality Type* by Jaroslaw Jankowski

# Additional information

## The four natural inclinations

1.  THE DOMINANT SOURCE OF LIFE
    ENERGY

    a.  THE EXTERIOR WORLD
        People who draw their energy
        from outside. They need activity
        and contact with others and find
        being alone for any length of time
        hard to bear.

    b.  THE INTERIOR WORLD
        People who draw their energy
        from their inner world. They need
        quiet and solitude and feel drained

when they spend any length of time in a group.

2. THE DOMINANT MODE OF ASSIMILATING INFORMATION

   a. VIA THE SENSES
People who rely on the five senses and are persuaded by facts and evidence. They have a liking for methods and practices which are tried and tested and prefer concrete tasks and are realists who trust in experience.

   b. VIA INTUITION
People who rely on the sixth sense and are driven by what they 'feel in their bones'. They have a liking for innovative solutions and problems of a theoretical nature and are characterised by a creative approach to their tasks and the ability to predict.

3. THE DOMINANT DECISION-MAKING MODE

   a. THE MIND
People who are guided by logic and objective principles. They are critical and direct in expressing their opinions.

b. THE HEART
People who are guided by their feelings and values. They long for harmony and mutual understanding with others.

4. THE DOMINANT LIFESTYLE

a. ORGANISED
People who are conscientious and organised. They value order and like to operate according to plan.

b. SPONTANEOUS
People who are spontaneous and value freedom of action. They live for the moment and have no trouble finding their feet in new situations.

# The approximate percentage of each personality type in the world population

| Personality Type: | Proportion: |
|---|---|
| • The Administrator (ESTJ): | 10-13% |
| • The Advocate (ESFJ): | 10-13% |
| • The Animator (ESTP): | 6-10% |
| • The Artist (ISFP): | 6-9% |
| • The Counsellor (ENFJ): | 3-5 % |
| • The Director (ENTJ): | 2-5% |
| • The Enthusiast (ENFP): | 5-8% |

- The Idealist (INFP):       1-4%
- The Innovator (ENTP):      3-5%
- The Inspector (ISTJ):      6-10%
- The Logician (INTP):       2-3%
- The Mentor (INFJ):         ca. 1%
- The Practitioner (ISTP):   6-9%
- The Presenter (ESFP):      8-13%
- The Protector (ISFJ):      8-12%
- The Strategist (INTJ):     1-2%

# The approximate percentage of women and men of each personality type in the world population

| Personality Type: | Women / Men: |
|---|---|
| The Administrator (ESTJ): | 40% / 60% |
| The Advocate (ESFJ): | 70% / 30% |
| The Animator (ESTP): | 40% / 60% |
| The Artist (ISFP): | 60% / 40% |
| The Counsellor (ENFJ): | 80% / 20% |
| The Director (ENTJ): | 30% / 70% |
| The Enthusiast (ENFP): | 60% / 40% |
| The Idealist (INFP): | 60% / 40% |
| The Innovator (ENTP): | 30% / 70% |
| The Inspector (ISTJ): | 40% / 60% |
| The Logician (INTP): | 20% / 80% |
| The Mentor (INFJ): | 80% / 20% |
| The Practitioner (ISTP): | 40% / 60% |
| The Presenter (ESFP): | 60% / 40% |
| The Protector (ISFJ): | 70% / 30% |
| The Strategist (INTJ): | 20% / 80% |

# Bibliography

- Arraj, Tyra & Arraj, James: *Tracking the Elusive Human, Volume 1: A Practical Guide to C.G. Jung's Psychological Types, W.H. Sheldon's Body and Temperament Types and Their Integration*, Inner Growth Books, 1988
- Arraj, James: *Tracking the Elusive Human, Volume 2: An Advanced Guide to the Typological Worlds of C. G. Jung, W.H. Sheldon, Their Integration, and the Biochemical Typology of the Future*, Inner Growth Books, 1990
- Berens, Linda V.; Cooper, Sue A.; Ernst, Linda K.; Martin, Charles R.; Myers, Steve; Nardi, Dario; Pearman, Roger R.; Segal, Marci; Smith, Melissa: *A. Quick Guide to the 16 Personality Types in Organizations: Understanding Personality Differences in the Workplace*, Telos Publications, 2002

- Geier, John G. & Downey, E. Dorothy: *Energetics of Personality*, Aristos Publishing House, 1989
- Hunsaker, Phillip L. & Alessandra, Anthony J.: *The Art of Managing People*, Simon and Schuster, 1986
- Jung, Carl Gustav: *Psychological Types (The Collected Works of C. G. Jung, Vol. 6)*, Princeton University Press, 1976
- Kise, Jane A. G.; Stark, David & Krebs Hirsch, Sandra: *LifeKeys: Discover Who You Are*, Bethany House, 2005
- Kroeger, Otto & Thuesen, Janet: *Type Talk or How to Determine Your Personality Type and Change Your Life*, Delacorte Press, 1988
- Lawrence, Gordon: *People Types and Tiger Stripes*, Center for Applications of Psychological Type, 1993
- Lawrence, Gordon: *Looking at Type and Learning Styles*, Center for Applications of Psychological Type, 1997
- Maddi, Salvatore R.: *Personality Theories: A Comparative Analysis*, Waveland, 2001
- Martin, Charles R.: *Looking at Type: The Fundamentals Using Psychological Type To Understand and Appreciate Ourselves and Others*, Center for Applications of Psychological Type, 2001
- Meier C.A.: Personality: *The Individuation Process in the Light of C. G. Jung's Typology*, Daimon Verlag, 2007

- Pearman, Roger R. & Albritton, Sarah: *I'm Not Crazy, I'm Just Not You: The Real Meaning of the Sixteen Personality Types*, Davies-Black Publishing, 1997

- Segal, Marci: Creativity and Personality Type: *Tools for Understanding and Inspiring the Many Voices of Creativity*, Telos Publications, 2001

- Sharp, Daryl: Personality Type: *Jung's Model of Typology*, Inner City Books, 1987

- Spoto, Angelo: *Jung's Typology in Perspective*, Chiron Publications, 1995

- Tannen, Deborah: *You Just Don't Understand*, William Morrow and Company, 1990

- Thomas, Jay C. & Segal, Daniel L.: *Comprehensive Handbook of Personality and Psychopathology, Personality and Everyday Functioning*, Wiley, 2005

- Thomson, Lenore: *Personality Type: An Owner's Manual*, Shambhala, 1998

- Tieger, Paul D. & Barron-Tieger Barbara: *Just Your Type: Create the Relationship You've Always Wanted Using the Secrets of Personality Type*, Little, Brown and Company, 2000

- Von Franz, Marie-Louise & Hillman, James: *Lectures on Jung's Typology*, Continuum International Publishing Group, 1971

**Putting the Reader first.**

An Author Campaign Facilitated by ALLi.

www.ingramcontent.com/pod-product-compliance
Lightning Source LLC
Chambersburg PA
CBHW031209020426
42333CB00013B/855